This Book Belongs To

................Tegan CHsp....Oak....year 5.

....

First published 2019 by Upfront Publishing, Peterborough, England

Copyright © Lindsey Bavin & Rebecca Rees, 2019.

All quotes from *The Book of Margery Kempe* are from the 2015 Oxford University Press edition translated by Anthony Bale.

ISBN: 978-178456-677   (Perfect Bound)

Other titles by the authors:

King's Lynn and The Hanseatic League by Rebecca Rees and Lindsey Bavin
A History of King's Lynn by Rebecca Rees

King's Lynn Minster

Project Funded By:

The Friends of True's Yard Fisherfolk Museum

Table of Contents

Foreword

Margery Kempe's book tells us about one of England's most important medieval women. Lynn was a major port in the 15th century and its merchants traded with the German Hanseatic cities and Bruges and Bordeaux; they even acted as bankers and ambassadors for the king. Margery's father was one such man. John Brunham was both mayor and member of parliament several times in the late 14th century. Her son John was a merchant in Hanseatic Danzig where he married a German woman whom Margery escorted back to the Baltic following his death in Lynn. The wealth generated by seaborne trade was invested in public buildings and private houses as well as churches which made Lynn a treasury of medieval architecture. Margery herself witnessed a great deal of this building work which can be admired in the town today.

Dr Paul Richards

The North End Trust Chairman

September 2019

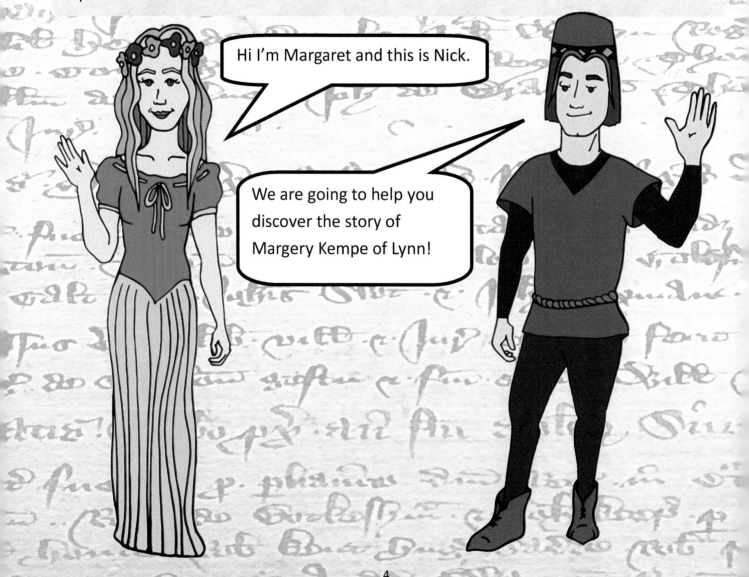

Introduction: Who was Margery Kempe?

So who was Margery Kempe and why is she important?

She was someone who was born and lived in King's Lynn (then called Bishop's Lynn) during the late 14th and early 15th centuries. Margery is important because *The Book of Margery Kempe* is the first **autobiography** written in English. Her story shows us what life was like for women in the **medieval** period.

Did You Know? Bishop's Lynn became King's Lynn in 1537 when Henry VIII split from the Roman Catholic Church and made himself the Supreme Head of the Church of England.

Glossary

Autobiography — A book about someone's life, written by that person.

Medieval — A period in European history from about 600 to 1500 AD.

Professor Anthony Bale

Executive Dean of Arts and Professor of Medieval Studies at Birkbeck, University of London. In 2015 Anthony published a new translation of *The Book of Margery Kempe*.

"Margery Kempe shows how England in the fifteenth century was connected to the wider world, from Lynn and Norwich to Jerusalem and Rome. Her Book is one of the earliest pieces of writing by and about women in the English language, and it describes lots of details of life in the past - including what people wore, what they ate, how they travelled across Europe, and what they believed. Margery Kempe was also at times brave, daring, and challenging, and The Book of Margery Kempe, which she had written down when she was in her 60s, is a unique window into life in the past."

Dr Laura Kalas Williams

Lecturer in Medieval Literature at Swansea University and co-founder of The Margery Kempe Society. Laura's book, *Margery Kempe's Spiritual Medicine*, will be published in 2020 .

"Margery Kempe's Book gives us a rare glimpse into what life was like for merchant class women in the Middle Ages. As well as being very religious, Margery Kempe was a businesswoman and well-known figure in her home town. She travelled the world, knew the content of lots of books, and was very brave, defending herself against many enemies. She was not afraid to speak out about what she believed in. Her Book shows us how women have always had key roles throughout history. She can inspire us to be ourselves and to fight for what we think is important. "

Kempe is so important?

Elizabeth MacDonald

Senior stocks editor of the FOX Business Network and author of *Skirting Heresy: The Life and Times of Margery Kempe*.

"The reason Margery Kempe is so important is because this daughter of a powerful mayor of Lynn gave us a gift with her memoirs, a richly detailed, real life Chaucer's Canterbury Tales. Margery detailed life during this time like never before. How she was arrested by the men who later helped orchestrate the execution of Joan of Arc. Her battles with the powerful Catholic Church are shockingly honest, as well as her stories of how she was repeatedly kicked out of pilgrimages. Most importantly, Margery was trying to explain deep inner problems and mysteries. What caught me was a feeling of a deep, rich stream of information in Margery's memoirs. Historians and academics often portray Margery as a histrionic, demanding, self-righteous, irritating woman. She is. But read her memoirs more closely, and you'll see a window into an extraordinary period in England —and of the men and women who reformed Christianity forever. People the world over can take great comfort in the gripping humanity and spirit of Margery's story."

Why I think Margery Kempe is important:

_____

_____

_____

_____

_____

_____

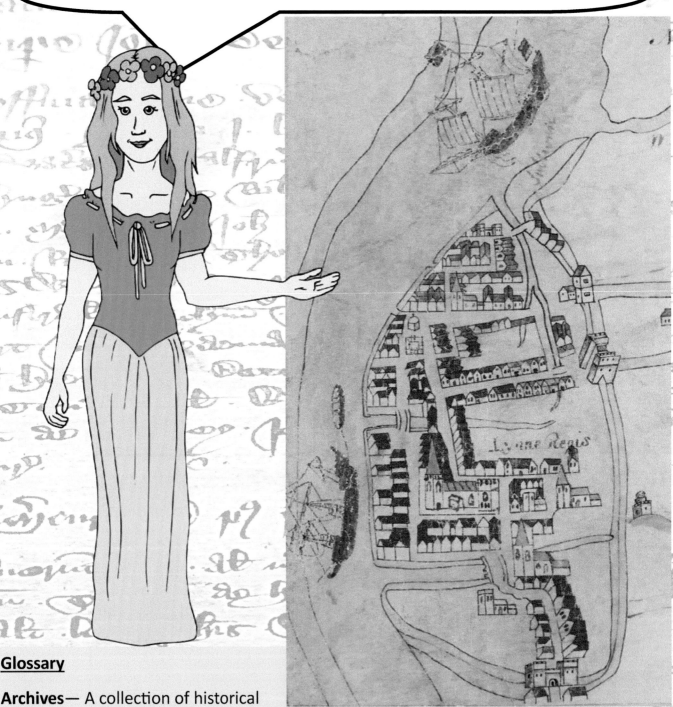

Margery also wrote about events which happened in Lynn's history, which gives us an idea of what the town was like then. Margery's Lynn probably wouldn't have looked too different from the Lynn shown in this map.

A copy of a 1588 map of Lynne Regis, Norfolk Record Office [BL 71].

Glossary

Archives— A collection of historical documents and records.

Merchant— Someone who buys and sells goods in large amounts.

The Red Register—An early paper book of 14th century Lynn legal documents kept at the Town Hall.

Fun Fact! Margery Kempe is remembered by the Church of England on 9th November.

Chapter One: Family

So, Margery, what was your family like?

My father, John Brunham, was a wealthy **merchant**, who was Mayor of Lynn five times between 1370 and 1391. He also represented Lynn in Parliament five times between 1365 and 1384.

Entry in **The Red Register** mentioning Margery's father, John Brunham (King's Lynn Borough **Archives**, KL/C 10/1 folio 135).

Did You Know? Margery was probably in her early 20s when she married another Lynn merchant, John Kempe. In the medieval period, however, it was not unusual for girls to be married much younger. In 1406 Princess Philippa of England sailed from Lynn on her way to be married to King Eric of Denmark, Norway and Sweden. She was 12 years old and he was about 24.

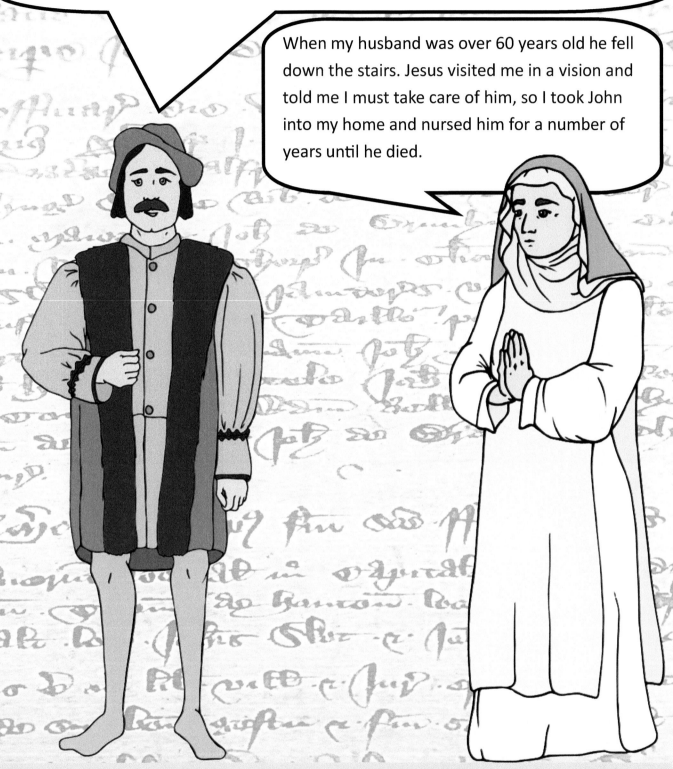

Margery was very proud of who her father was, but she didn't feel quite the same about me, her husband, John Kempe. I was a **burgess** of Lynn, but never became Mayor like her father. We eventually lived separately after Margery said she would rather see someone chop off my head than sleep in the same bed as me!

When my husband was over 60 years old he fell down the stairs. Jesus visited me in a vision and told me I must take care of him, so I took John into my home and nursed him for a number of years until he died.

Glossary

Burgess—A person who had full rights of citizenship in a town (in medieval England people did not have equal rights).

Gdańsk— A Polish city on the Baltic coast.

From her book we know Margery had 14 children! Unfortunately in the medieval period a lot of children died young—so it is unlikely that all Margery's children lived to adulthood.

In the past childbirth was very dangerous for women and many of them died because of it.

Did You Know? One of Margery's children was called John Kempe (like his father). He moved to Danzig (now called **Gdańsk**), where he married a local woman and had a daughter. He died while visiting Lynn with his wife and Margery then accompanied her daughter-in-law back to Danzig. In 2015 a letter from John Kempe was discovered in Gdańsk.

Unfortunately, apart from mentioning her father, husband and son, Margery did not leave any details about the rest of her family. References to the Brunham and Kempe families in the King's Lynn Borough Archives allow a possible family tree to be created. As you can see there is still a lot we don't know!

My book was more about my religious life than my family. Besides, when I had a vision of the Virgin Mary and she offered me a seat in Heaven near Jesus, I said I wanted to take my parish priest, Robert Spryngold, with me instead of my father, husband or children.

Did You Know? It is much more difficult to discover information about medieval women than men, as women don't often appear in records. A mention of Isabelle de Brunham in a 1410 **Will** probably refers to Margery's mother, but it is impossible to be sure. Unfortunately we don't have the Wills of Margery or any of her close family, which would have given us more information.

Glossary

Will—A legal document which says who you want to leave everything you own to when you die.

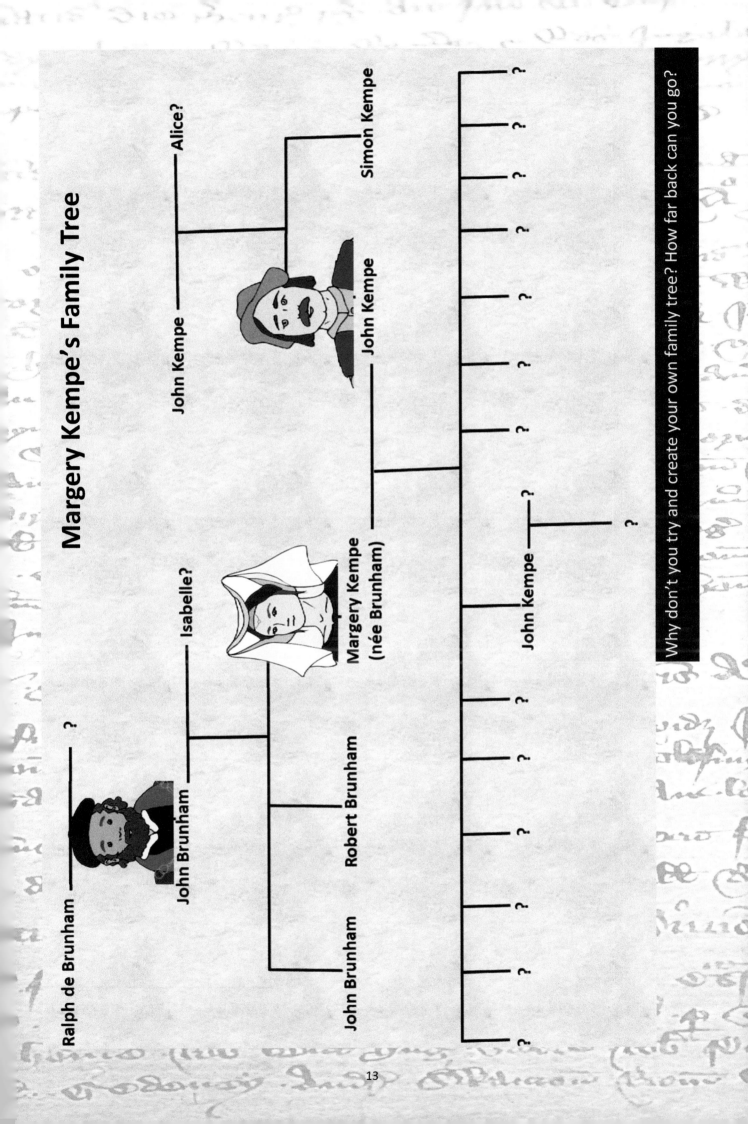

Margery Kempe's Family Tree

Ralph de Brunham —— ?

John Brunham —— Isabelle?

John Brunham —— ?

Robert Brunham

Margery Kempe (née Brunham) —— John Kempe —— Alice?

John Kempe

Simon Kempe

John Kempe —— ?

Why don't you try and create your own family tree? How far back can you go?

13

Sadly we don't know what Margery looked like. However, she did leave a description of the expensive clothes she liked to wear when she was younger.

"...she wore gold piping on her headdress, and her hoods were **dagged** with **tippets**. Her cloaks were also dagged and lined with many colours between the dags, so it would be more striking to people's eyes and she herself should be more admired."

Glossary

Dagged— A cut away pattern at the bottom of an item of clothing which shows a different colour fabric underneath.

Elaborate— Something which is more detailed and complicated.

Tippets— Long strips of material which hung down from the elbow of the sleeve of a dress.

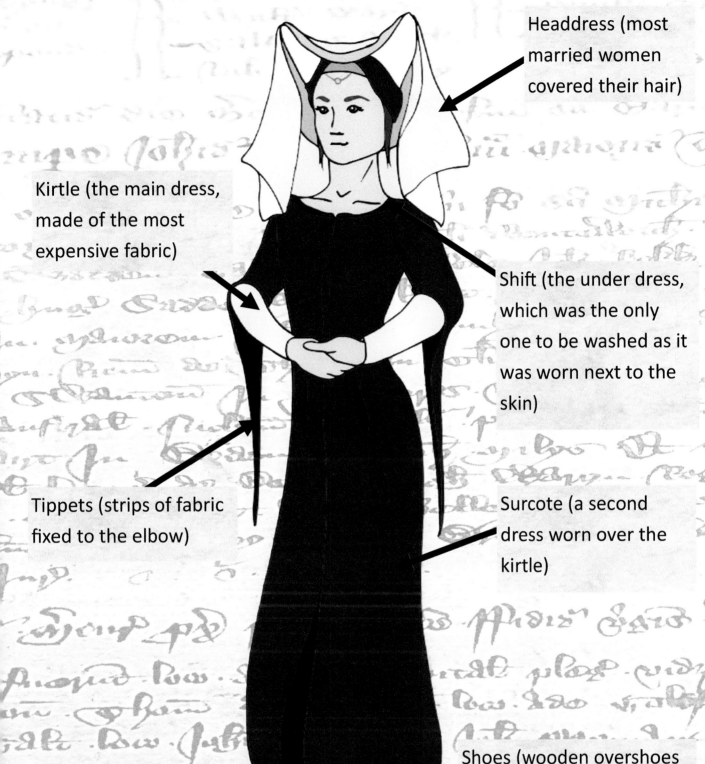

Headdress (most married women covered their hair)

Kirtle (the main dress, made of the most expensive fabric)

Shift (the under dress, which was the only one to be washed as it was worn next to the skin)

Tippets (strips of fabric fixed to the elbow)

Surcote (a second dress worn over the kirtle)

Shoes (wooden overshoes called pattens could be worn on top of your normal shoes if it was muddy outside)

Hose (worn by men and women, they were a bit like socks, but had to be tied, usually just below the knee, to stop them falling down).

Did You Know? In the medieval period once a woman was married she had to wear a headdress to cover her hair. By Margery's time these had started to get more **elaborate**, with wire used to create interesting shapes.

Chapter Two: Visions

Margaret, when you say Margery had visions what do you mean?

A vision is the **perception** of something other people cannot see.

Margery's first vision was shortly after the birth of her first child. Having a baby can be upsetting and can leave mothers feeling **mentally** unwell. In her book we hear how she fell ill for '*half a year, eight weeks and some odd days*'. Without help, **mental** health can worsen and Margery would not have had access to the kind of help you can find today. Margery's vision was followed by more visions of horrible things and voices telling her to hurt herself. At the end of this period of illness she had another vision but this time a positive one.

Glossary

Forsaken/Forsook— Left behind or abandoned.

Mental/Mentally— Something to do with the mind.

Perception—Being aware of something using your senses (sight, hearing, taste, touch and/or smell).

But Margaret, if no one else could see them does that mean Margery was mad?

Nick, that is not a nice thing to say. Anyone can become mentally unwell, even you. Many people in Margery's time thought that she was ill. But many also believed that she truly experienced visions of God. If you saw a rabbit in a field but it hopped away before your friend could see it does that mean the rabbit wasn't there, or that you are lying or mad?

No. It just means <u>they</u> didn't see it.

Precisely. It is not nice to be called mad or a liar. Margery was called many nasty names because she had visions. That must have made her feel very sad at times.

Glossary

Abbess— A woman who is head of an Abbey where nuns live.

Anchoress— A religious woman who lives in seclusion.

Great Schism — The split between the Eastern Orthodox Church and Roman Catholic Church.

Heresy– A belief or act that is against the rules of the Church.

Latin— The language of the ancient Romans and the Roman Catholic Church.

Mystic— Someone who claims to have had contact with God.

Nunneries— Buildings where nuns live.

Did You Know? If you ever feel unwell mentally or physically it is important to let someone know.

Although my visions may be considered unusual, in the Medieval World it was not uncommon. I would sometimes cry so loudly whenever I felt God's love that they even gave me my own chapel in St Margaret's Church to pray in so I wouldn't disturb everyone else.

Saint Hildegard of Bingen was a 12th Century German **Abbess** and author of several works including *Divine Ways* and *On God's Activity*. She was just 3 years old when she had her first vision. When she was 8 her parents gave her to the church as an **oblate**. She went on to become an Abbess and founded two **nunneries**.

Marguerite Porete was a 13th Century Belgian **Mystic** and author of the *Mirror of Simple Souls*. She was burned for **heresy** in 1310 because her book was written in Old French and not **Latin**.

Julian of Norwich was a 14th Century **Anchoress** and author of *Revelations of Divine Love*. Like Margery she was seriously ill when she had her first vision and she lived a long life. However, unlike Margery she was an anchoress which meant she could not leave her room and lived alone with only a cat for company.

Saint Catherine of Siena was a 14th Century Italian mystic, ambassador, author, doctor and **oracle**. After her parents tried to marry her at 15 she cut off her hair in protest and then caught smallpox. She had her first vision aged 20, was the first woman to be made a doctor of the Church, advisor to two Popes and made several predictions including the **Great Schism**. After her death in Rome the people of Siena tried to steal her severed head so she could be buried there but upon being challenged by Roman guards found the bag to contain only rose petals.

Sister Catherine was a German Medieval Mystic—her first vision was had after everyone thought she had been dead for 3 days but then awakened claiming to have experienced unity with God.

Glossary

Oblate—Someone dedicated to doing God's work.

Oracle—Someone thought to give wise advice and be able to see the future.

There are lots of different **theories** as to why Margery saw things other people could not. We will take a look at some of them.

Her visions were real religious experiences.

Postpartum psychosis.

She made them up.

Side effect of fasting.

Epilepsy.

Ergotism.

Glossary

Absences— When you lose awareness of your surroundings for a short period of time.

Exorcism—A religious practice to remove an evil spirit from someone's body.

Convulsions—Muscles contract and relax quickly making the body move uncontrollably.

Gangrene—When blood flow to an area of the body is cut off and it starts to rot.

Hallucinations—Seeing, hearing, smelling, tasting or feeling things that aren't there.

Possessed— A person believed to be controlled by an evil spirit.

Margery's Visions—The Theories

Her visions were real – See the list of other Medieval Mystics on page 19.

Postpartum psychosis – 'Post' means 'after' and 'partum' means 'birth'. Psychosis is a form of mental illness with **symptoms** such as **hallucinations** and uncontrollable crying which Margery was infamous for.

She made them up—Possible, but dangerous, as her actions left her open to accusations of heresy or being **possessed** by the devil.

Side effect of fasting—Fasting is when you limit the amount you eat and drink for a period of time for religious reasons. This could have resulted in Margery having low blood sugar the symptoms of which can include tearfulness, weakened eyesight, **seizures** and nightmares.

Epilepsy—An illness which results in seizures of varying kinds from **absences** to full body **spasms**. It was a known condition and it is mentioned in Margery's book but she discounts it.

Ergotism– Eating grains that have been infected by a fungus. The symptoms include visions and **convulsions** but it is unlikely Margery suffered from ergotism because she lived a long life and did not appear to suffer from **gangrene**.

We will never really know the truth about Margery's visions, but she honestly believed they were real.

What do you think?

Glossary

Seizures—See Convulsions.

Spasms—See Convulsions.

Symptoms—A sign of illness.

Theories– Ideas not yet proven as facts.

Did You Know? There is a 4,000-year-old Babylonian Tablet in the British Museum which accurately described the symptoms of different types of epileptic seizures. Unfortunately, the treatment recommended was an **exorcism**. ..

Although during my lifetime there were many people who didn't believe my visions were real, there were some who did, like my good friend Alan of Lynn. Sadly the head of the White Friars in England heard about our friendship and ordered Master Alan to stop seeing me. When Master Alan later became very ill I prayed to God to cure him and he did! After that we were allowed to speak to each other again.

I believed that Margery's visions and uncontrollable crying were signs that God was talking to her. I also believed her survival after being hit by a falling stone and wooden beam in St Margaret's Church was a **miracle**!

Glossary

Miracle– Something which can't be explained by science and is usually seen as an act of God.

Quench— Put out.

Margery's Miracles

Margery was praying in St Margaret's Church when a stone and part of a wooden beam fell from the ceiling and onto her head and back. She cried out to Jesus and suddenly the pain was gone and she was unharmed.

The priest who wrote down Margery's story had difficulty reading an early draft written by someone else (the handwriting was terrible and the writer's English and German was very bad). Margery prayed to God and the priest suddenly found the book easier to read. However, his eyesight was failing and he could no longer see to write, so Margery prayed again and he was able to see.

So what do you think: were Margery's experiences miracles or not?

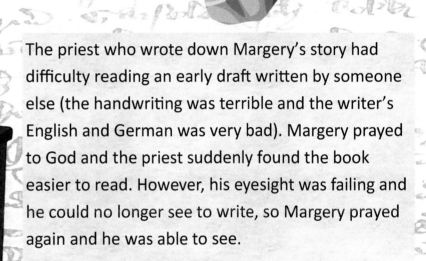

The Trinity Guildhall on the Saturday Market Place went up in flames and sparks started coming into St Margaret's Church. Margery called out to God to *"send some rain down or some weather...that may **quench** this fire"*. It then started to snow and the Church was saved.

Chapter Three: Pilgrimages

Margaret, what is **pilgrimage**? Is it a type of bird?

No Nick, but that's a good guess. A pilgrimage is a journey to a place of **religious significance**. Take a look at this map at all the places Margery visited.

Glossary

Pilgrimage– A journey to visit a religious site or object.

Religious– Holy.

Significance– Important meaning.

Key:

Margery's First Pilgrimage (1413-1415) ————

Margery's Second Pilgrimage (1417-1418) ▬▬▬

Margery's Third Pilgrimage (1433-1434) ▬▬▬

Facts about Margery's Journeys

- Margery's first journey was shortly after the loss of her father, John Brunham, in October 1413. She did not return until Easter 1414.

- Margery sometimes travelled alone which was very unusual for the time. This was because the pilgrim parties she joined often left her behind because of her crying (they even took her maidservant with them).

- Women like Margery had to get written permission from their husbands to travel.

- She caught lice.

- She was so shocked when she first saw Jerusalem she nearly fell off her donkey.

- When she made her final pilgrimage she was around 60 years old.

Margery didn't always follow the guidebook. We know on her pilgrimage to Rome she largely ignored the famous sites instead preferring to spend time with the poorest people in the city and seek out places where her idol St Bridget of Sweden may have gone.

This way to the Colosseum

Fun Fact! Pilgrims collected badges of the holy sites they had been to. Sometimes they were said to contain holy water or the blood of a saint.

Pilgrim Badges from Lynn Museum.

Pilgrimage Advisor

Read Reviews, Compare Relics, Book.

Venice is at '*the height of its medieval splendour, rich in commerce and holy relics.*'

Reviewed 1415

Margery Kempe, Bishop's Lynn, Norfolk, England

'*Many people in Rome…asked her to dinner and gave her a very warm welcome*'.

Reviewed 1415

Margery Kempe, Bishop's Lynn, Norfolk, England

In Jerusalem '*great grace and spiritual comfort that she had felt when she was there*', but at the River Jordan '*the weather was so hot that she believed her feet should burn*'.

Reviewed 1415

Margery Kempe, Bishop's Lynn, Norfolk, England

This creature '*had a pleasant time* [in Santiago de Compostela], *both physically and spiritually*'.

Reviewed 1418

Margery Kempe, Bishop's Lynn, Norfolk, England

This creature was '*warmly welcomed by many people*' in Danzig.

Reviewed 1434

Margery Kempe, Bishop's Lynn, Norfolk, England

The 'Lenn Ship' (King's Lynn Borough Archives, KL/C2/35)

Things To Do On Pilgrimage

1. Visit Shrines such as Walsingham or Thomas Becket's Tomb.

2. Buy **indulgences** – Margery bought these for herself, her friends, enemies and even for the souls of people in **purgatory** who she didn't know .

3. Look at holy **relics**—There was quite a bit of money to be made from tourism. So much so that St Anne (Jesus' grandmother) apparently had 7 heads—the 7 places that claimed to have her head were all recognised by the church as sacred relics.

4. Get a tattoo—Normally a cross. It was believed that if you were attacked by bandits you just had to show them your tattoo, pay a fee and they would be set you free.

5. Buy pilgrim badges. Each shrine would have a different symbol that could be understood even by people who couldn't read or write. The symbols were:

A). A small bottle of oil (St Thomas Becket at Canterbury)

B). A shell (Santiago de Compostela in Spain)

C). A palm leaf (Jerusalem)

D). Crossed keys (Rome)

I travelled with my husband to Canterbury to visit the tomb of Thomas Becket, but he went off somewhere and left me alone. Some of the people and monks of Canterbury wanted to burn me!

It was only for a day and only because you wouldn't stop crying! How was I supposed to know that was going to happen? Besides it's not as bad as the time you went to the Holy Land and annoyed the people you were travelling with so much they cut off the bottom part of your dress and then left you behind in Constance!

Glossary

Indulgences—Little pieces of paper that pardoned sins and reduced the amount of time a soul would have to spend in purgatory.

Purgatory—A place where , according to the Roman Catholic faith, souls wait until their sins are forgiven and they can go into Heaven.

Relics—Objects with links to a holy person (often body parts!).

Chapter Four: Margery's Book

Is it really true that Margery didn't write her own book?

Yes it is! At that time most people were **illiterate** and those who could read and write were usually men, or women who were either from the **aristocracy** or who lived in nunneries. Margery had to rely on others to read to her and write down her autobiography as she talked.

Glossary

Aristocracy— The highest class in society, usually people of noble birth.

Confessor—A priest who listens to people saying what they have done wrong.

Illiterate— Unable to read or write.

It took me a few attempts to get my book written. My first attempt was with an Englishman, living in Germany, who was staying with me while in Lynn. Unfortunately, he died before the book was complete, and the next two people to make the attempt had difficulty reading what he'd already written. His handwriting was terrible!

I'm Robert Spryngold, Margery's **confessor** and parish priest of St Margaret's Church in Lynn. Many people think I wrote Margery's book for her.

Did You Know? Many people think the person who first tried to write down Margery's story was her son, John Kempe Jnr., as Margery's mention of Germany refers to an area much larger than Germany today and probably included the part of present day Poland where her son was living.

I've been trying to read Margery's book, but it doesn't make sense! I don't understand it!

The Book of Margery Kempe is written in Middle English. This is an older version of the English language we speak today and can sometimes be a bit difficult to understand. Remember they didn't have dictionaries in the medieval period, so there was no set way of spelling words!

Did You Know? At this time most books and legal documents were written in Latin or French. Latin was the language of the Church and French had been the language of the English aristocracy since the Norman Conquest in 1066.

Ye Olde Guide to Middle English

Middle English	Modern English
Buxom	Obedient
Boisterous/Boistous	Hard, heavy, or big
Damsel	A young woman
Dewchman	A German (many Germans lived in Lynn during Margery's lifetime)
Caytyf	A wretched, miserable person
Pompows	Showy, luxurious
Stokfysch	Stockfish, a dried fish and common food in Margery's Lynn.
Vexyd	Troubled
Wroth	Anger
Xal	Shall (a Norfolk word)
Ypocrit	Hypocrite

Fun Fact! Margery's book is not only written in Middle English, it also has a Norfolk accent!

So was Margery the only woman creating her own book at this time?

No, she wasn't. She wasn't even the first woman to produce a book written in English—that was done by me, Julian of Norwich. I wrote *Revelations of Divine Love* from my anchorite's cell in the Church of St Julian in Norwich.

Did You Know? An anchorite's cell was attached to a church and the anchoress would decide to go inside and be sealed in. There would be small openings to allow them to talk to people and receive food. They would not leave the cell for the rest of their life. We don't even know Julian's real name, as she was known after the church where her cell was. All Saints Church in King's Lynn also once had an anchorite cell attached to it.

Fun Fact! Margery Kempe visited Norwich and spoke to Julian of Norwich. She made sure to record the meeting in her book.

So what happened to Margery's book once it was written?

Well, no one really knows, but copies of it were made. Unfortunately, all but one 15th century copy of her book, written by me, Richard Salthouse, have been lost or destroyed. The only one which survived is now in The British Library, and it has quite an interesting story...

Fun Fact! After this copy of Margery's book was written some of its later owners, probably monks or nuns, wrote comments in the book's margins. That wasn't all they wrote—someone recorded a recipe for a type of sweet called *confits* or *dragges*, which could be taken as medicine. See how to make a modern version of these on page 53.

What happened?

It was lost and then rediscovered in the 1930s during a party at the home of the Butler-Bowden family in Derbyshire. The book was lying forgotten in a cupboard! In 1934 a medieval historian called Hope Emily Allen announced that it had been identified as a long lost copy of *The Book of Margery Kempe*.

The book was sold to The British Library in 1980.

Did You Know? Until this copy of Margery Kempe's book was found all historians had of it were parts which had been printed in a seven page booklet by London publisher Wynkyn de Worde in 1501.

Chapter Five: Margery's World

Margaret, what was life like for medieval men and women?

That's a great question Nick! The thing is life was very different depending on your class.

That makes sense—my life is very different if I've had a maths class. I'm terrible at maths!

No Nick, I mean if they were rich or poor.

Glossary

Fast —Going without food for a period of time for religious reasons.

Haircloth—Material usually made from rough horsehair and worn for religious reasons.

Plague— A deadly illness which spreads quickly and easily.

How can you tell?

Well Nick, take someone like me, Margery's father, for example. I was a wealthy merchant and Mayor of Lynn. So Margery and I would have been well dressed and well fed. People with less money were not so lucky.

However, when I got older I chose to wear plainer clothes and to **fast**. I even chose to wear a **haircloth** under my clothes, which would have been very scratchy! This was meant to be uncomfortable and be a contrast to my rich lifestyle.

Did You Know? After the Black Death of 1348-49 there were regular outbreaks of **plague** in England. This caused millions of deaths throughout Europe and no one was safe, no matter what their class. Even King Edward III lost a daughter, Joan, in 1348. She was 14 years old and died in France while on her way to Spain to marry Peter/Pedro of Castile (who, when he became King, was known as 'the Just' and also 'the Cruel'!).

If you wanted to learn to read and write the best path for a Medieval woman was to become a nun.

Being a nun meant:

- You could never marry or have children (unless you were a widow—which meant your husband was dead).

- You would have to spend the rest of your life in a nunnery.

- Your life would be spent in prayer, contemplation and work.

So why didn't Margery just become a nun?

Well as you can see, there were a few...problems!

Nun Eligibility Quiz

Do you have?

Husband ☑

Children ☑

Desire to travel ☑

If you selected any of the above you can't be a nun.

Glossary

Eligibility- A test to see if you can do a certain job.

> No Nick- a revolt is a form of protest. The peasants just wanted to be paid fairly for their hard work.

Why did the Peasants' Revolt?

- **Serfs** worked for 5-6 days a week for their Lord then the rest of the time had to work their own fields for food.

- They were often not paid for their work but still had to pay taxes themselves.

- There was a tax you had to pay to get married, have a baby, if there was a war, etc. As they didn't have money this mostly took the form of crops or livestock.

- They couldn't leave. If the land was sold to another landowner, they were sold with it.

Margery would have been only 8 years old. Peasants from Bishop's Lynn joined the rebellion and fought at the Battle of North Walsham against the heavily armed forces of the Bishop of Norwich, Henry le Despenser. It was the last major battle of the rebellion and the 'King of the Commons' Geoffrey Litster was captured. Wat Tyler, leader of the rebellion, was tricked and also captured, bringing about the end of the revolt.

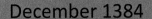

Breaking News—John Wycliffe condemned as a heretic by Pope Urban VI!

That's terrible! What had he done?!

He thought the Bible should be in English so everyone could understand it. He also believed there should be an end to **perpetual serfdom** which made him unpopular with the lords and barons.

Although Margery was only 11, this event would have a huge impact later on in her life. Wycliffe's followers were known as **Lollards** and were **persecuted** in The Heresy Trials. Young Margery was not a fan of Pope Urban VI because he agreed that St Nicholas' Chapel should have a font!

Glossary

Lollards—Followers of the teachings of John Wycliffe.

Perpetual—Never ending.

Persecuted—When someone is badly treated because of their religious or political beliefs.

Serfdom/Serfs—Being bound to working the land of an estate.

1400

Breaking News—England at War with France and Scotland!

Henry IV asked the Hanseatic League not to trade or help France and Scotland. They refused and trouble broke out in Hanseatic cities, like Danzig, where many English merchants lived. The English merchants accused the Hanseatic merchants of seizing their ships and stealing their cargo!

So what did Henry IV do then?

Henry IV issued a royal licence to allow merchant ships from Lynn and other east coast ports to attack Hanseatic, French and Scottish ships. In essence the King gave permission for people like me to commit acts of piracy!

Introducing John Brandon

A Lynn merchant who exported cloth, hides and grain, and imported soap, garlic, herring, eels and sturgeon. He led a fleet of English ships (called cogs) to attack foreign ships during this Sea War and The Hanseatic League saw him as England's chief pirate. John Brandon, however, went on to become Mayor of Lynn in 1409 and the last record of him was in 1413.

So did Margery know John Brandon?

Well, they were in Lynn at the same time, and Margery was a former Mayor's daughter so it is likely that they knew each other.

Introducing Klaus Störtebeker

While Margery may have been acquainted with John Brandon she certainly was not with this fellow. This German pirate was the terror of the North and Baltic Seas and commanded a crew of 73. He loved a fight and if a crew of a captured vessel surrendered without agreeing to one he'd have them thrown overboard! Unlike John Brandon, Störtebeker did not have permission to be a pirate and attacked ships from both his own country and others.

Fun Fact! In 1578 16 men were accused of piracy and tried in St George's Guildhall. Four were taken to the South Gate and hanged while the other 12 were taken to Norwich.

Did You Know? It wasn't just boys who turned to piracy. Princess Awilda became a pirate in the 5th century after her father tried to force her to marry Prince Alf of Denmark. They sent Prince Alf to deal with some troublesome pirates who were terrorising the coast, not realising it was Awilda and her crew. She was so impressed by his courage that she agreed to marry him.

2nd March 1401

Breaking News—Bishop's Lynn Priest William Sawtry burned for heresy!

Margery was 28 years old when William Sawtry, former priest at Margery's own St Margaret's Church, was the first person to be burned in England for heresy. Sawtry believed the Bible should be accessible to all and that the Church's enormous wealth should be spent on looking after the poor and the sick. Sounds reasonable enough?

Did You Know? Of all of Sawtry's beliefs the one that actually got him convicted of heresy was that the bread and wine in **communion** did not turn into Jesus's body and blood after the priest had blessed it.

1414

Breaking News—The Lollards are revolting!

I'm not falling for that one again!

Glossary

Communion– A religious ceremony where bread and wine are consumed and believed to become or represent the body and blood of Jesus.

Lollard knights led by Sir John Oldcastle rebelled against Henry V. The rebellion failed. Oldcastle escaped but was captured, tried and executed in 1417. Lollardy went underground.

Margery on Trial

Margery was accused of heresy by Archbishop Arundel, and for being in league with Sir John Oldcastle. She was arrested many times. Had she been found guilty she could have shared the same fate as William Sawtry.

1421

Breaking News—Fire in Bishop's Lynn. Holy Trinity Guildhall burned to the ground!

This was Margery's famous miracle- she prayed for an end to the fire that threatened her beloved St Margaret's Church and a snow storm put out the fire.

Timeline

The life and times of Margery Kempe.

1320	Margery's grandfather, Ralph de Brunham, was mentioned in Lynn's Red Register.
1337	The Hundred Years' War started between England and France.
1342	Julian of Norwich was born.
1348	The Black Death arrived in England.
1370	Margery's father, John Brunham, served his 1st term as Mayor of Lynn.
1373	Margery Brunham was probably born during this year in Lynn.
	On 8th May Julian of Norwich had a series of 16 visions.
1377	Edward III died and was succeeded by his 10 year old grandson, Richard II.
	John Brunham served his 2nd term as Mayor of Lynn.
1378	John Brunham served his 3rd term as Mayor of Lynn.
	Pope Urban VI granted St Nicholas' Chapel permission to hold baptisms, a decision Margery disagreed with.
1381	The Peasants' Revolt.
1385	John Brunham served his 4th term as Mayor of Lynn.
1386	John Brunham was appointed to prepare the men of Lynn for a possible French invasion.
1387	Geoffrey Chaucer's *The Canterbury Tales* were published.
1391	John Brunham served his 5th term as Mayor of Lynn.
c1393	Margery Brunham married John Kempe.
	Friar John Capgrave, an Augustinian friar and author, was born in Lynn.
1399	Richard II was overthrown by Henry IV.
1401	William Sawtry, former priest of St Margaret's Church in Lynn, was burnt at the stake for heresy in London.
1406	Princess Philippa (aged 12) sailed from Lynn to marry King Eric of Denmark, Norway and Sweden (aged about 24).
1413	Margery and John Kempe visited Yorkshire. They were interviewed by the Bishop of Lincoln and later by the Archbishop of Canterbury in London.
	Margery met Julian of Norwich.
	Henry IV died and was succeeded by Henry V.
c1413-15	Margery went on pilgrimage visiting Norwich, Great Yarmouth, Zierikzee, Constance, Bologna, Venice, the Holy Land, Venice (again), Assisi, Rome and Middelburg, before returning to Norwich.

1415	Henry V led his army to victory against the French in the Battle of Agincourt.
c1416	Last known record of Julian of Norwich
1417-18	Margery went on pilgrimage to Santiago de Compostela (sailing from and to Bristol).
	Margery visited Leicester, where she was arrested and questioned.
	Margery visited York and was questioned by the Archbishop of York at Cawood.
	Margery visited Bridlington and Hull. She was arrested and imprisoned in Beverley. The Archbishop of York questioned her (again).
	Margery visited Lincoln and London. She returned to Lynn via Ely.
1421	The Holy Trinity Guildhall on Saturday Market Place burnt down.
1422	Henry V died and was succeeded by his nine month old son, Henry VI.
1429	Pope Martin V withdrew permission for St Nicholas' Chapel to hold baptisms.
	The French, led by Joan of Arc, defeated the English at the Siege of Orléans.
1431	On 30th May Joan of Arc was burnt at the stake by the English.
	Margery's son, John Kempe, died in Lynn, while visiting his family. He had been living in Danzig (now Gdańsk).
	Margery's husband, also called John Kempe, died in Lynn.
1432	An application by St Nicholas' Chapel for permission to perform baptisms was denied because the Chapel did not have a font.
1433-34	Margery accompanied her daughter-in-law back to Danzig. They travelled via Norwich, Ipswich and Norway.
	Margery travelled from Danzig to Stralsund, Bad Wilsnack, Aachen, Calais, Dover, Canterbury and London.
1436	On 23rd July a cleric started making a copy of Book One of Margery's autobiography (he was the 3rd person to attempt it).
1438	On 28th April the same cleric started to write down Book Two of Margery's autobiography.
c1438	Margery Kempe died.
1440	Margaret de Mauteby married John Paston. She went on to become one of the key authors of the Paston Letters, documenting the rise of the family from Paston in Norfolk.
1453	The Hundred Years' War ended (after 116 years).
1455	The Wars of the Roses between the families of York and Lancaster over the English crown began.

Activities

Robert Spryngold's Word Search

E	P	M	E	K	M	B	Z	V	Y	E	P	Y	N	Z
W	V	Z	H	U	R	K	W	S	G	M	K	A	F	L
L	Z	W	Z	U	W	Y	E	A	Q	F	U	T	M	H
C	W	W	N	F	G	R	M	Q	A	T	M	W	A	J
W	D	H	J	X	E	I	H	C	O	F	K	J	R	Z
E	A	D	Q	H	R	A	U	B	O	U	G	F	G	R
M	L	H	I	G	X	H	I	Y	I	R	C	E	E	O
Z	F	C	L	H	P	O	H	S	I	B	H	C	R	A
Z	X	I	A	I	G	E	F	Q	J	Z	V	U	Y	F
V	P	G	O	R	L	L	A	H	D	L	I	U	G	F
Z	E	R	A	N	I	I	D	A	N	Z	I	G	Q	M
U	E	P	T	K	Z	M	R	E	M	O	R	F	K	O
M	H	J	I	W	K	B	J	D	W	T	M	J	T	O
Y	K	P	H	J	V	I	H	T	I	B	J	L	W	N
Y	J	I	N	P	K	P	N	N	Y	L	B	R	Z	H

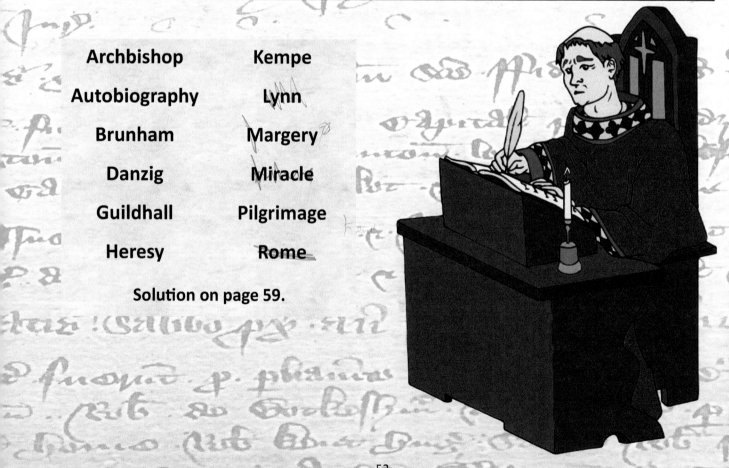

Archbishop   **Kempe**

Autobiography   **Lynn**

Brunham   **Margery**

Danzig   **Miracle**

Guildhall   **Pilgrimage**

Heresy   **Rome**

Solution on page 59.

Margery Kempe's Confits Recipe

The recipe that was added to f. 124 of *The Book of Margery Kempe* by a later medieval reader, and revealed by Dr Laura Kalas Williams, is for medicinal sweets called 'dragges', or 'confits'. The recipe instructs the reader to "*take Sugar candy, sugar plate* [sugar paste], *sugar with Aniseed, fennel seed, nutmeg, cinnamon, Ginger comfetes* [sugar covered ginger] *and licorice* [liquorice]. *Beat them together in a mortar and make them in all manner of food and drinks and dry first and last eat it.*"

> Well that reads like a technical challenge on The Great British Bake Off... Luckily Dr Theresa Tyer from Swansea University has come up with a version you can do at home!

Fun Fact! The use of sugar and spices in this recipe shows that whoever wrote it lived somewhere with plenty of money, as these ingredients would have been expensive in the 15th and 16th centuries.

Ingredients

3 grms of Tragacanth gum (E413)

35 mls of filtered water

225 grms of white icing sugar

2 level tsps. each of ground cinnamon, nutmeg, aniseed, fennel seed, and ginger

Extra icing sugar for dusting.

Please remember to check that whoever you are making this with is not allergic to any of these ingredients.

Don't forget—stage 1 of the recipe needs to be prepared the night before.

1. Put the gum granules into a bowl and add the water – stir and leave overnight to swell.

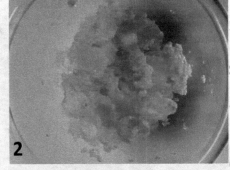

2. In the morning the gum granules you prepared earlier should be well-swollen and moist and there should be no residual water in the bowl. Test by squeezing between the fingers to make sure they are soft all the way through like frogspawn!

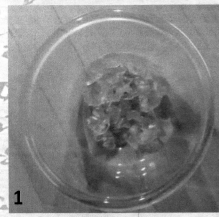

3. Put the icing sugar into a bowl with the spices and mix together.

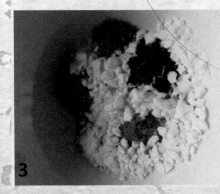

4. Gently sift the mixture (making sure that it doesn't fly everywhere!) so that it's well blended.

5. Gradually add the sugar and spice mix to the gum, blending it together to make sure there are no lumps. Keep adding the sugar until you have a paste that is neither too dry nor too sticky.

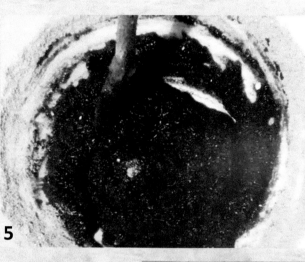

6. Turn the paste out onto a board – sprinkled with icing sugar – and kneed it until you have a soft pliable paste similar to bread or play-dough.

7. Roll the paste to approx. 1 cm thickness and then cut into strips and then squares so that each piece is about the same size.

8. Roll the pieces in the palm of the hands into a ball (cover the mixture

waiting to be rolled with a slightly damp cloth). Set the "confits" out on a piece of greaseproof paper, dust with icing sugar and leave in a warm, dry place to harden.

Sweets like these would have been eaten at the end of a meal to settle your stomach—a bit like the mints they give you in restaurants!

Fun Fact! The sugar and spice in the recipe are probably meant to represent the sweetness and warmth of God's love.

Margery Kempe's Town Trail

Map Key

1. Town Hall (Trinity Guildhall)

2. King's Lynn Minster (St. Margaret's Church)

3. The Hanse House

4. King's Lynn Ferry

5. St. George's Guildhall

6. St. Nicholas' Chapel

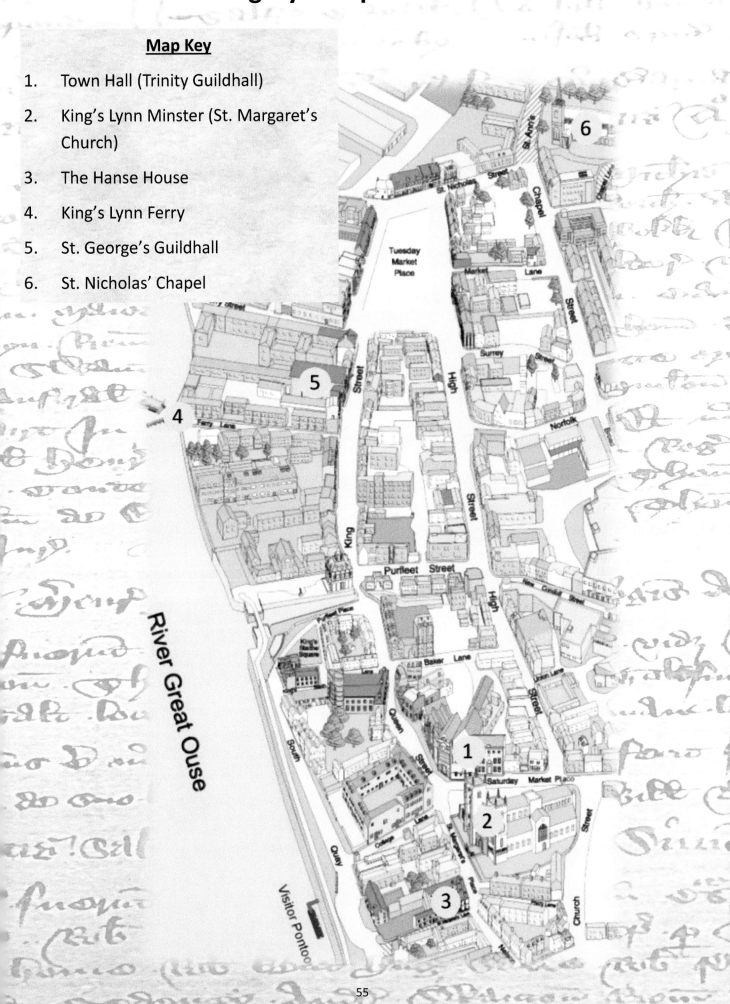

1). Start in the Saturday Market place. The Town Hall was the Trinity Guildhall in Margery's time and the last reference to her is her name in the membership list of the Holy Trinity Guild. We know this building was built after 1421 because Margery describes the previous Guildhall burning down in a fire!

2). Go inside King's Lynn Minster. In Margery's book she describes a number of events which take place inside this Church (see page 23). Some of the Church is very different to how it was in Margery's time. The nave (where the pews are) was larger, but in 1741 the Church's spire fell down and destroyed it.

3). Leave the church, cross the road and walk down St Margaret's Lane, beside the Hanse House. This is the only surviving Hanseatic warehouse in the country. The Hanseatic League was a trading organization made up of German cities and towns and Lynn was one of their trading partners. From ports like Lynn trading networks spread throughout Europe and German and English ships allowed Margery to travel on her pilgrimages and her son to move to Danzig.

As you walk along the quayside towards the Custom House imagine how the river would have looked in Margery's time—full of wooden ships (called cogs) from all over Europe. They brought in lots of different goods, like stockfish (wind-dried cod) from Norway, which Margery mentions in her book. Can you find the stockfish sculpture on the quayside?

The 'Lenn Ship' (King's Lynn Borough Archives, KL/C2/35)

4). When you reach the Custom House walk down King Street (Stockfish Row in Margery's time). Go down Ferry Lane to the King's Lynn Ferry landing. There has been a ferry service across the river for over 700 years and for much of that time it was the only way to cross. Margery and her husband would have used the ferry service when leaving the town on some of their journeys.

As you walk back onto King Street take a look at the timber framed building on the other side of the road (No. 28-32). This gives you an idea of what most buildings in Lynn would have looked like in Margery's lifetime.

5). Continue along King Street to St. George's Guildhall. Built in the 1420s it would have been a familiar sight to Margery, especially as it was built in brick, which was unusual at that time.

6). Cross Tuesday Market Place and head towards St. Nicholas' Chapel. The Chapel's spire was blown down during a storm in 1741, but was replaced because it was used by sailors as a landmark to help them navigate the river into Lynn. Landmarks which are used like this are known as seamarks.

Before you go into the Chapel have a look around the graveyard for the little white cottage beside the gate. This is The Exorcist's House. An exorcist was a priest who cast out demons and devils which they thought were living in someone's body or house. Some people in Margery's time would have thought she needed to see an exorcist.

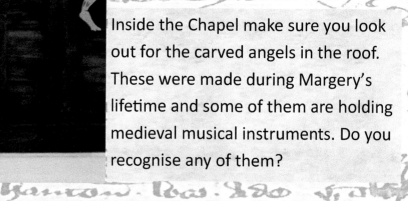

Inside the Chapel make sure you look out for the carved angels in the roof. These were made during Margery's lifetime and some of them are holding medieval musical instruments. Do you recognise any of them?

Other places in Lynn you can visit with links to Margery Kempe are:

115-117 High Street—The site of the Brunham family home, where Margery probably grew up.

St James Chapel ruins (near the entrance to The Walks, opposite the Police Station) — Margery records in her book that she went to the Chapel to listen to a famous friar preach, but was turned away because she was crying too loudly.

The Whitefriars Gate (Friars Walk)—This is all that remains of the friary where Margery's friend and advisor Alan of Lynn lived. She was considered a bad influence and for a time they were forbidden to talk to each other.

Robert Spryngold's Word Search Solution

E	P	M	E	K	M	B	Z	V	Y	E	P	Y	N	Z
W	V	Z	H	U	R	K	W	S	G	M	K	A	F	L
L	Z	W	Z	U	W	Y	E	A	Q	F	U	T	M	H
C	W	W	N	F	G	R	M	Q	A	T	M	W	A	J
W	D	H	J	X	E	I	H	C	O	F	K	J	R	Z
E	A	D	Q	H	R	A	U	B	O	U	G	F	G	R
M	L	H	I	G	X	H	Y	I	R	C	E	E	O
Z	F	C	L	H	P	O	H	S	I	B	H	C	R	A
Z	X	I	A	I	G	E	F	Q	J	Z	V	U	Y	F
V	P	G	O	R	L	L	A	H	D	L	I	U	C	F
Z	E	R	A	N	I	I	D	A	N	Z	I	G	Q	M
U	E	P	T	K	Z	M	R	E	M	O	R	F	K	O
M	H	J	I	W	K	B	J	D	W	T	M	J	T	O
Y	K	P	H	J	V	I	H	T	I	B	J	L	W	N
Y	J	J	I	N	P	K	P	N	N	Y	L	B	R	Z	H

So how did you do?

Did you know that in the medieval period most women, including me, were not taught how to read or write? Instead they had to rely on others to do it for them!

Colouring In

Glossary

Abbess	A woman who is head of an Abbey where nuns live.
Absences	When you lose awareness of your surroundings for a short period of time.
Anchoress	A religious woman who lives in seclusion.
Archives	A collection of historical documents and records.
Aristocracy	The highest class in society, usually people of noble birth.
Autobiography	A book about someone's life, written by that person.
Burgess	A person who had full rights of citizenship in a town (in medieval England people did not have equal rights).
Communion	A religious ceremony where bread and wine are consumed and believed to become or represent the body and blood of Jesus.
Confessor	A priest who listens to people saying what they have done wrong.
Convulsions	Muscles contract and relax quickly making the body move uncontrollably.
Dagged	A cut away pattern at the bottom of an item of clothing which shows a different colour fabric underneath.
Elaborate	Something which is more detailed and complicated.
Eligibility	A test to see if you can do a certain job.
Exorcism	A religious practice to remove an evil spirit from someone's body.
Fast	Going without food for a period of time for religious reasons.
Forsaken	Left behind or abandoned.
Forsook	See Forsaken.
Gangrene	When blood flow to an area of the body is cut off and it starts to rot.
Gdańsk	A Polish city on the Baltic coast.
Great Schism	The split between the Eastern Orthodox Church and Roman Catholic Church.
Haircloth	Material usually made from rough horsehair and worn for religious reasons.
Hallucinations	Seeing, hearing, smelling, tasting or feeling things that aren't there.
Heresy	A belief or act that is against the rules of the Church.
Illiterate	Unable to read or write.
Indulgences	Little pieces of paper that pardoned sins and reduced the amount of time a soul would have to spend in purgatory.
Latin	The language of the ancient Romans and the Roman Catholic Church.
Lollards	Followers of the teachings of John Wycliffe.

Medieval	A period in European history from about 600 to 1500 AD.
Mental	Something to do with the mind.
Mentally	See Mental.
Merchant	Someone who buys and sells goods in large amounts.
Miracle	Something which can't be explained by science and is usually seen as an act of God.
Mystic	Someone who claims to have had contact with God.
Nunneries	Buildings where nuns live.
Oblate	Someone dedicated to doing God's work.
Oracle	Someone thought to give wise advice and be able to see the future.
Perception	Being aware of something using your senses (sight, hearing, taste, touch and/or smell).
Perpetual	Never ending.
Persecuted	When someone is badly treated because of their religious or political beliefs.
Pilgrimage	A journey to visit a religious site or object.
Plague	A deadly illness which spreads quickly and easily.
Possessed	A person believed to be controlled by an evil spirit.
Purgatory	A place where , according to the Roman Catholic faith, souls wait until their sins are forgiven and they can go into Heaven.
Quench	Put out.
Relics	Objects with links to a holy person (often body parts!).
Religious	Holy.
Seizures	See Convulsions.
Serfdom	Being bound to working the land of an estate.
Serfs	See Serfdom.
Significance	Important meaning.
Spasms	See Convulsions.
Symptoms	A sign of illness.
Theories	Ideas not yet proven as facts.
The Red Register	An early paper book of 14th century Lynn legal documents kept at the Town Hall..
Tippets	Long strips of material which hung down from the elbow of the sleeve of a dress.
Will	A legal document which says who you want to leave everything you own to when you die.

List of Illustrations

Front cover: King's Lynn Minster, courtesy of Tim Rees.

Page backgrounds: King's Lynn Borough Archives, KLC 101, folio 135, image used with permission of the Norfolk Record Office. Photograph by John Self.

Coat of Arms of King's Lynn & West Norfolk, courtesy of the Borough Council of King's Lynn & West Norfolk.

Dr Paul Richards, image courtesy of Alison Gifford.

Professor Anthony Bale, Dr Laura Kalas Williams & Elizabeth MacDonald, images provided by the individuals.

Map of Lynne Regis, Norfolk Record Office [BL 71] *'BL71: Undated [19th century] copy of 1588 map of western Norfolk from King's Lynn to Flitcham showing Castle Rising Chase'*, image courtesy of Norfolk Record Office.

King's Lynn Borough Archives, KLC 101, folio 135, image used with permission of the   Norfolk Record Office. Photograph by John Self.

Map of Europe from http://www.free-largeimages.com/map-of-europe-752/.

Pilgrim Badges, used with kind permission of Lynn Museum, Norfolk Museums Service.

King's Lynn Borough Archives, KL/C2/35, image courtesy of the Norfolk Record Office.

Medieval Confits images, courtesy of Dr Theresa Tyers.

Discover Lynn map of the Town Centre, used with kind permission of The Borough   Council of King's Lynn & West Norfolk Tourism Section.

King's Lynn Town Hall, courtesy of Isobel Rees.

King's Lynn Minster, courtesy of Tim Rees.

The Hanse House, used with kind permission of Kirsty Gauntley.

King's Lynn Borough Archives, KL/C2/35, image courtesy of the Norfolk Record Office.

Stockfish sculpture, courtesy of Rebecca Rees.

28-32 King Street, courtesy of Rebecca Rees.

St George's Guildhall, courtesy of Rebecca Rees.

St Nicholas Chapel, courtesy of Rebecca Rees.

St Nicholas Chapel Angel Roof, courtesy of Tim Rees.

Skirting Heresy picture, courtesy of Elizabeth MacDonald.

Colleen O'Brien, image provided by the individual.

Lindsey Bavin, image provided by the author.

Rebecca Rees, courtesy of Isobel Rees.

Selected Bibliography

Alsford, S. (2017) *Biographies of Lynn townsmen* [online]. Available at: <http://users.trytel.com/~tristan/towns/biography/biolynn.html> [Accessed 09/08/2018].

Arnold, J.H. and Lewis, K.J. eds. (2004) *A Companion of Margery Kempe.* Boydell & Brewer Ltd.

Flood, A. (2015) *Archive find shows medieval mystic Margery Kempe's autobiography 'doesn't lie'* [online]. Available at: <https://www.theguardian.com/books/2015/may/08/archive-find-shows-medieval-mystic-margery-kempes-autobiography-doesnt-lie> [Accessed 24/04/2018].

Gertz, G. (2012) *Heresy Trials and English Women Writers, 1400-1670*, Cambridge University Press

Goodman, A. (2002) *Margery Kempe and Her World.* Pearson Education Ltd.

Julian of Norwich (1998) *Revelations of Divine Love*. Translated by Elizabeth Spearing, introduction by A.C. Spearing. Penguin.

Kean, D. (2017) *Recipe found in medieval mystic's writings was probably for 'dragges'* [online]. Available at: <https://www.theguardian.com/books/2017/feb/28/recipe-found-in-medieval-mystics-writings-was-probably-for-drugges-margery-kempe> [Accessed 24/04/2018].

Kelliher, H. (1997) *The Rediscovery Of Margery Kempe: A Footnote* [online] British Library Journal. Available at: <http://www.bl.uk/eblj/1997articles/pdf/article19.pdf> [Accessed 07/08/2018].

Kempe, M. (2015) *The Book of Margery Kempe* Translated by Anthony Bale. Oxford University Press.

Kempe, M. (1996) *The Book of Margery Kempe* [online]. Edited by Lynn Staley . Medieval Institute Publications. Available at <https://d.lib.rochester.edu/teams/publication/staley-the-book-of-margery-kempe> [Accessed 22/03/2019]

MacDonald, E. (2014) *Skirting Heresy: The Life and Times of Margery Kempe*. Franciscan Media.

Raguin, V. and Stanbury, S. (2009) Mapping Margery Kempe [online]. Available at: <http://college.holycross.edu/projects/kempe/pilgrimage/europemap.htm> [Accessed 23/10/2018].

Scott Stokes, C. (1999) *Margery Kempe's Family Background and Early Years, 1373–1393*. Mystics Quarterly, 25 (March/June 1999) [online]. Available at: <http://college.holycross.edu/projects/kempe/text/familybg.html> [Accessed 10/08/2018].

Williams, Laura Kalas, (2018) The Swetenesse of Confection: A Recipe for Spiritual Health in London, British Library, Additional MS 61823, The Book of Margery Kempe. Studies in the Age of Chaucer Vol. 40: 155-190 (The New Chaucer Society).

Williams, Laura Kalas, (2020) *Margery Kempe's Spiritual Medicine: Suffering, Transformation and the Life-Course* (Boydell and Brewer).

Index

Acknowledgements

The authors would like to extend their thanks to the following people:

The trustees, staff, friends and volunteers at True's Yard Fisherfolk Museum for their help and support during this project. Particularly Dr Paul Richards (The North End Trust) and John Self (The Friends of True's Yard Museum).

Their families for their patience, understanding and support.

Luke Shackell at King's Lynn Borough Archives for his assistance in locating documents relating to Margery Kempe and her family.

The advice and support offered by Professor Anthony Bale (whose wonderful 2015 translation of *The Book of Margery Kempe* has been invaluable), in particular the selection of Middle English words on page 35.

Dr Laura Kalas Williams for sharing her research on the recipe in *The Book of Margery Kempe* and agreeing to proof read this book!

Susan Maddock for her advice in the early stages of this project and sharing her knowledge of Margery Kempe's Lynn.

Dr Theresa Tyers for her hours of research and experimentation in creating a modern version of the recipe for confits.

Josh Elms and the team and volunteers at Wellbeing Norfolk and Waveney.

Mr Kevin Wales and the children of the 2019-20 Year 5 Rowling Class at St Edmund's Academy in King's Lynn for their help proof reading the book and highlighting words that needed to be included in the glossary.

The numerous organizations and individuals who provided images for this book and in particular to Colleen O'Brien for her brilliant illustrations.

About the Margery Kempe Project

SKIRTING HERESY - THE LIFE AND TIMES OF MARGERY KEMPE

Skirting Heresy: The Life and Times Of Margery Kempe, by Elizabeth MacDonald was performed in King's Lynn Minster on 22nd September 2018. The play was directed by Christopher Yarnell and the cast managed by Jan Sayer—Former Stage Manager of the Sydney Opera House. The play focuses on Margery's life and trial for heresy—how she was nearly burned at the stake for her beliefs and visions!

The cast was internationally diverse, much like the Lynn of Margery's lifetime. The part of Margery was played by Emily Blake actress, singer, presenter and plus sized model.

An original score was created by Gareth Calway, Andy Wall and Vanessa Wood-Davies of the Penland Phezants—the play was performed where Margery worshiped and probably buried. It was a once in a lifetime experience!

The play was a community project and funded by extensive fundraising on Crowdfunder. Costumes were provided by the Maddermarket Theatre in Norwich and paid for by a grant from the Norfolk Arts Project Fund.

About True's Yard Fisherfolk Museum

True's Yard Fisherfolk Museum is run by The North End Trust, which was founded by Pat Midgley in 1989. The Museum itself opened in 1991 and celebrated its 25th anniversary in 2016. The Museum has expanded twice due to Heritage Lottery Funding and now consists of several buildings including the tea room, fisherfolk cottages, smithy, smokehouse, education room and research centre.

About the Illustrator

Colleen O'Brien is a Canadian national who grew up in the United States. She graduated in 2019 completing a Bachelor of the Arts with Honours at Norwich University of the Arts where she achieved a First-Class mark. She is currently going on to complete a Master of the Arts at the University of Brighton.

About the Authors

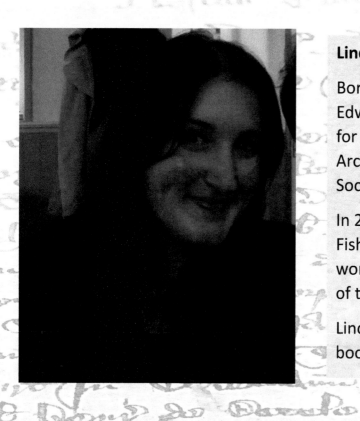

Lindsey Bavin:

Born in Lynn, Lindsey went to school at King Edward VII. She moved away in 2004 to study for her BA Hons in Ancient History and Archaeology and MA in Myth and Ancient Society.

In 2012 she became involved with True's Yard Fisherfolk Museum through volunteering and worked her way up to becoming the manager of the Museum.

Lindsey is also the co-author of the children's book; *King's Lynn and the Hanseatic League* .

Rebecca Rees:

Rebecca was born in King's Lynn and attended Rosebery Avenue First School, Gaywood Junior School and Springwood High School. She studied at Newcastle University for a BA (Hons) in Classical Studies and an MA in Heritage Education and Interpretation.

Rebecca is Deputy Manager of True's Yard Fisherfolk Museum, Project Manager for The Marriott's Warehouse Trust and a member of the King's Lynn Town Guides. She is also the co-author of the children's book; *King's Lynn and the Hanseatic League* and author of *A History of King's Lynn*.